EMMANUEL JOSEPH

Guiding Light, Teaching Morals, Faith, and Business Acumen to the Next Generation

Copyright © 2025 by Emmanuel Joseph

All rights reserved. No part of this publication may be reproduced, stored or transmitted in any form or by any means, electronic, mechanical, photocopying, recording, scanning, or otherwise without written permission from the publisher. It is illegal to copy this book, post it to a website, or distribute it by any other means without permission.

First edition

This book was professionally typeset on Reedsy.
Find out more at reedsy.com

Contents

1	Chapter 1: The Foundation of Morals	1
2	Chapter 2: The Role of Faith in Personal Growth	3
3	Chapter 3: Cultivating Empathy and Compassion	5
4	Chapter 4: The Power of Integrity in Business	7
5	Chapter 5: Overcoming Adversity with Resilience	9
6	Chapter 6: The Importance of Lifelong Learning	11
7	Chapter 7: Leading with Humility	13
8	Chapter 8: Building Trust Through Transparency	15
9	Chapter 9: Ethical Decision-Making in Business	17
10	Chapter 10: The Impact of Community Service	19
11	Chapter 11: The Role of Mentorship in Personal Development	21
12	Chapter 12: Balancing Ambition with Ethical Values	23
13	Chapter 13: The Power of Gratitude	25
14	Chapter 14: The Importance of Work-Life Balance	27
15	Chapter 15: Inspiring the Next Generation	29

1

Chapter 1: The Foundation of Morals

The journey to success begins with a strong moral foundation. At the core of every individual's character lies a set of values that guide their actions and decisions. Honesty, integrity, empathy, and compassion are essential building blocks that shape ethical behavior. Imagine a young entrepreneur named David, who, despite facing financial hardship, chose to operate his business with transparency and fairness. His unwavering commitment to honesty not only earned him the trust and loyalty of his customers but also set a powerful example for his peers. David's story demonstrates that when we prioritize our morals, we create a ripple effect that positively impacts those around us.

In a small village, there lived an elderly woman named Mrs. Thompson, known for her unwavering integrity. She ran a modest grocery store where she would often give away food to those in need, even when it meant sacrificing her own profits. One cold winter, a family struggling to make ends meet entered her store, desperate for help. Without hesitation, Mrs. Thompson provided them with enough provisions to last through the season. Word of her generosity spread throughout the village, inspiring others to follow her example. This story highlights how acts of kindness and integrity can foster a sense of community and create a lasting impact.

Empathy and compassion are crucial components of a moral life. They allow us to connect with others on a deeper level and understand their experiences. Take the story of Emily, a young teacher who noticed one of her students, Sarah, struggling with her studies. Instead of reprimanding her, Emily took the time to understand the challenges Sarah faced at home. She discovered that Sarah's parents were going through a difficult divorce, which affected her academic performance. By showing empathy and offering additional support, Emily helped Sarah regain her confidence and succeed in school. This example illustrates the importance of compassion in nurturing others and fostering their growth.

Another powerful example of moral character comes from a successful businessman named Robert. Despite the competitive nature of his industry, Robert always prioritized ethical practices. When faced with a lucrative opportunity that involved cutting corners, he chose to uphold his principles and declined the offer. His decision not only safeguarded his company's reputation but also earned him the respect of his colleagues and competitors. Robert's story serves as a reminder that maintaining integrity in all aspects of life, especially in business, can lead to long-term success and fulfillment.

2

Chapter 2: The Role of Faith in Personal Growth

Faith is a powerful force that shapes our values and guides our decisions. It provides a sense of purpose and direction, especially during challenging times. For many, faith is the anchor that keeps them grounded and resilient. Consider the story of Maria, who faced the sudden loss of her job due to company downsizing. In her moment of despair, Maria turned to her faith for strength and clarity. Through prayer and reflection, she found the courage to start her own small business. With hard work and determination, Maria's venture flourished, and she eventually became a source of inspiration for her community. Her story illustrates how faith can be a guiding light in our darkest moments.

In another instance, a young man named Daniel relied on his faith to overcome adversity. Growing up in a challenging environment, Daniel faced numerous obstacles that could have led him astray. However, his strong belief in his faith provided him with a moral compass and a sense of hope. With the support of his church and community, Daniel pursued higher education and eventually became a mentor to at-risk youth. By sharing his experiences and the role of faith in his journey, Daniel helped others find their own paths to success. His story underscores the transformative power of faith in personal growth and resilience.

Faith can also foster a sense of community and belonging. In a bustling city, a group of individuals from diverse backgrounds came together to form a community center based on shared values and faith. This center became a safe haven for those seeking guidance, support, and connection. Through various outreach programs, they provided resources and assistance to those in need, creating a strong network of support. One heartwarming story from this community involves a single mother, Lisa, who found herself overwhelmed by life's challenges. The community center offered her emotional and financial support, helping her regain stability and confidence. This example demonstrates how faith-based communities can create a positive impact on individuals and society.

The role of faith extends beyond personal struggles; it also influences our professional lives. Take the case of James, an entrepreneur who built his business on the principles of his faith. He prioritized ethical practices, fair treatment of employees, and giving back to the community. Despite facing tough competition, James's business thrived because of his commitment to these values. His employees felt valued and motivated, and his customers appreciated the integrity and purpose behind his products. James's story highlights how integrating faith into our professional endeavors can lead to success and fulfillment while making a positive impact on those around us.

3

Chapter 3: Cultivating Empathy and Compassion

Empathy and compassion are essential traits that enable us to connect with others on a deeper level. They allow us to understand and share the feelings of those around us, fostering a sense of community and support. One compelling story involves a young girl named Ava, who noticed her classmate, Tom, often sitting alone during lunch. Sensing his loneliness, Ava reached out to Tom, inviting him to join her group of friends. Over time, their friendship blossomed, and Tom's confidence grew. Ava's act of kindness not only changed Tom's life but also inspired her classmates to be more inclusive and empathetic.

In another story, a medical student named Michael volunteered at a local clinic in an underserved community. He quickly realized that many patients felt unheard and misunderstood. Michael made it his mission to listen to their stories and address their concerns with genuine compassion. His efforts led to improved patient outcomes and a stronger bond between the clinic and the community. Michael's experience taught him that empathy and compassion are crucial components of effective healthcare and can lead to transformative change.

Compassion can also be a driving force in social entrepreneurship. Consider the story of Maya, who founded a company that produces affordable, eco-friendly sanitary products for women in low-income regions. Motivated by the struggles of women in her community, Maya's compassion drove her to create a sustainable solution that addressed their needs. Her company not only provided essential products but also offered employment opportunities, empowering women and improving their quality of life. Maya's story highlights the impact of compassion in creating positive social change.

A touching story of empathy involves a young boy named Liam, who noticed that his elderly neighbor, Mr. Jenkins, struggled with maintaining his garden. Despite his busy schedule, Liam offered to help Mr. Jenkins with gardening tasks every weekend. Over time, they developed a strong friendship, and Liam learned valuable life lessons from Mr. Jenkins. This story illustrates how small acts of empathy can lead to meaningful connections and enrich our lives.

4

Chapter 4: The Power of Integrity in Business

Integrity is the bedrock of ethical business practices. It involves being honest, transparent, and accountable in all dealings. One exemplary story is that of Sarah, a small business owner who prioritized quality over profits. When she discovered a flaw in one of her products, Sarah immediately issued a recall and offered refunds to her customers. Her transparency and commitment to quality earned her customers' trust and loyalty, ultimately leading to her business's long-term success.

In another instance, a startup founder named Alex faced a dilemma when a potential investor proposed a lucrative deal that required compromising his company's ethical standards. Despite the financial allure, Alex chose to uphold his principles and declined the offer. His decision preserved the integrity of his brand and attracted investors who shared his values. Alex's story demonstrates that integrity can be a powerful differentiator in the business world.

Consider the story of a multinational corporation that faced a major scandal due to unethical practices. The new CEO, Maria, took swift action to address the issues, implementing rigorous ethical guidelines and fostering a culture of accountability. Her leadership not only restored the company's reputation but also set a new standard for integrity in the industry. Maria's efforts highlight the importance of integrity in building and sustaining a successful business.

A heartwarming story of integrity comes from a local bakery owned by a couple, John and Emma. One day, they accidentally received an overpayment from a customer. Instead of keeping the extra money, they contacted the customer and returned the amount. The customer's gratitude led to positive word-of-mouth, and the bakery gained a reputation for its honesty and integrity. John and Emma's story shows that even small acts of integrity can have a significant impact on a business's success.

5

Chapter 5: Overcoming Adversity with Resilience

Resilience is the ability to bounce back from challenges and setbacks. It is a crucial trait for navigating life's uncertainties. Consider the story of Jessica, a promising athlete who suffered a severe injury that jeopardized her career. Instead of giving up, Jessica dedicated herself to a rigorous rehabilitation program. With determination and perseverance, she not only recovered but also returned to compete at an even higher level. Jessica's story exemplifies the power of resilience in overcoming adversity.

In another story, a young entrepreneur named Mark faced numerous obstacles while launching his tech startup. From funding shortages to technical glitches, Mark encountered setbacks at every turn. However, his resilience and problem-solving skills enabled him to navigate these challenges and ultimately create a successful product. Mark's journey underscores the importance of resilience in achieving entrepreneurial success.

Resilience can also be seen in the story of a community that faced a natural disaster. After a devastating hurricane, residents came together to rebuild their homes and support one another. Their collective resilience and solidarity not only restored the community but also strengthened their bonds. This story highlights the power of resilience in overcoming collective challenges and fostering a sense of unity.

A heartening example of resilience involves a single mother, Lisa, who lost her job and faced financial hardship. Determined to provide for her children, Lisa enrolled in a vocational training program and secured a new job in a different industry. Her resilience and determination allowed her to create a better future for her family. Lisa's story illustrates how resilience can empower individuals to overcome personal challenges and achieve their goals.

6

Chapter 6: The Importance of Lifelong Learning

Lifelong learning is the continuous pursuit of knowledge and skills throughout one's life. It is essential for personal and professional growth. One inspiring story is that of Robert, a retired engineer who decided to learn a new language. Through dedication and practice, Robert became fluent in Spanish and used his newfound skills to volunteer as a translator for a non-profit organization. His story demonstrates that it is never too late to embrace lifelong learning and make a positive impact.

In another instance, a young professional named Rachel pursued a series of online courses to enhance her skills in digital marketing. Her commitment to lifelong learning led to a promotion and new career opportunities. Rachel's story highlights the benefits of continuous learning in staying competitive and achieving career success.

Consider the story of a community center that offers free educational programs for individuals of all ages. From coding workshops to art classes, the center provides opportunities for lifelong learning and skill development. One heartwarming story from the center involves an elderly woman named Margaret, who discovered a passion for painting and showcased her artwork at a local gallery. Margaret's experience illustrates the joy and fulfillment that lifelong learning can bring.

A compelling example of lifelong learning comes from a company that encourages its employees to pursue further education and professional development. One employee, Tom, took advantage of this opportunity and completed a leadership training program. His new skills and knowledge enabled him to take on a managerial role, contributing to the company's success. Tom's story underscores the importance of lifelong learning in personal and organizational growth.

7

Chapter 7: Leading with Humility

Humility is a key trait of effective leadership. It involves recognizing and valuing the contributions of others and fostering a collaborative environment. One notable story is that of Emma, a project manager who always credited her team's efforts for their success. By leading with humility, Emma created a positive work culture that motivated her team to excel. Her leadership style not only improved team performance but also earned her the respect and admiration of her colleagues.

In another instance, a CEO named Daniel faced a major crisis that threatened his company's future. Instead of blaming others, Daniel took responsibility and sought input from his team to find solutions. His humility and willingness to listen empowered his employees to contribute their ideas and expertise, ultimately resolving the crisis. Daniel's story highlights the importance of humility in navigating challenging situations and fostering a collaborative work environment.

Consider the story of a school principal, Mrs. Johnson, who always took the time to listen to her students' concerns and ideas. Her humility and approachability created a nurturing environment where students felt valued and heard. One memorable story involves a student council member, Sarah, who proposed a new initiative to promote mental health awareness. Mrs. Johnson's support and encouragement helped bring Sarah's idea to life, benefiting the entire school community. This story illustrates how humility can enhance leadership effectiveness and create positive outcomes.

A heartwarming example of leading with humility comes from a non-profit organization led by a director named Mark. Mark often participated in volunteer activities alongside his team, demonstrating his commitment to their mission. His humility and hands-on approach inspired his team to work passionately towards their goals. Mark's story shows that leading with humility can foster a sense of unity and purpose within an organization.

8

Chapter 8: Building Trust Through Transparency

Transparency is essential for building trust in both personal and professional relationships. It involves being open, honest, and clear in communication and actions. One notable story is that of a tech company that faced a data breach. The CEO, Laura, addressed the issue with complete transparency, informing customers of the breach and the steps being taken to rectify the situation. Her honesty and accountability helped rebuild customer trust and loyalty. Laura's story underscores the importance of transparency in maintaining trust and credibility.

In another instance, a non-profit organization faced financial difficulties and had to make tough decisions regarding its programs. The executive director, Michael, held a series of town hall meetings to openly discuss the challenges and solicit input from staff and stakeholders. His transparency fostered a sense of shared responsibility and led to innovative solutions that stabilized the organization. Michael's story highlights the positive impact of transparency in navigating difficult situations.

Consider the story of a family-owned business that prioritized transparency in its operations. The owners, John and Lisa, regularly shared financial updates and business plans with their employees. This openness created a culture of trust and collaboration, where employees felt valued and invested in the company's success. One memorable story involves an employee, Maria, who suggested a cost-saving measure that significantly improved the company's profitability. John and Lisa's commitment to transparency empowered their team to contribute to the business's growth.

A compelling example of transparency comes from a local government initiative aimed at improving public infrastructure. The city council held regular community meetings to discuss project plans, budgets, and timelines. They also provided online updates and responded to residents' questions and concerns. This level of transparency built trust between the government and the community, leading to greater public support and cooperation. One memorable story involves a neighborhood that, thanks to the transparent communication, actively participated in a beautification project, resulting in a vibrant and cohesive community space.

A heartwarming story of transparency involves a couple, Jack and Emily, who decided to be completely open with their children about their financial situation. When Jack lost his job, they sat down with their kids and explained the challenges they were facing. The family worked together to make budget cuts and find creative ways to save money. This honesty and openness not only strengthened their family bond but also taught their children valuable lessons about financial responsibility and resilience.

9

Chapter 9: Ethical Decision-Making in Business

Ethical decision-making is crucial for long-term success in business. It involves considering the impact of decisions on all stakeholders and choosing actions that align with one's values. One exemplary story is that of a pharmaceutical company that faced a dilemma when it discovered a potential side effect of a newly developed drug. Despite the financial implications, the company chose to halt the drug's release and conduct further research to ensure its safety. Their commitment to ethical decision-making preserved their reputation and demonstrated their dedication to patient well-being.

In another instance, a tech startup named Innovatech faced pressure from investors to prioritize profits over ethical practices. The founder, Lisa, stood firm in her commitment to sustainability and fair labor practices. She implemented eco-friendly production methods and ensured fair wages for all employees. Her ethical decisions not only attracted like-minded investors but also built a loyal customer base that appreciated the company's values. Lisa's story highlights the importance of staying true to one's principles in the face of external pressures.

Consider the story of a retail company that encountered a supplier offering products at significantly lower prices. However, upon investigation, the company discovered that the supplier engaged in unethical labor practices. Instead of compromising their values for higher profits, the company chose to source from ethical suppliers, even at a higher cost. Their commitment to ethical decision-making earned them respect and loyalty from consumers who valued responsible business practices.

A heartwarming example of ethical decision-making comes from a family-owned restaurant. When a supplier delivered subpar ingredients, the owners, Sarah and Tom, decided to temporarily close the restaurant rather than serve their customers inferior meals. They openly communicated the situation to their patrons and ensured that only the highest-quality ingredients were used when they reopened. Sarah and Tom's dedication to quality and ethics strengthened their customers' trust and loyalty.

10

Chapter 10: The Impact of Community Service

Community service is a powerful way to demonstrate moral values and give back to society. It fosters a sense of belonging and creates positive change. One inspiring story is that of a group of high school students who organized a clean-up drive in their neighborhood. Their efforts not only improved the local environment but also brought the community together. The students' initiative inspired others to participate in similar projects, creating a lasting impact on their community.

In another instance, a corporate team volunteered at a local shelter, providing meals and support to homeless individuals. Their dedication and compassion made a significant difference in the lives of the shelter residents. One touching story involves a volunteer named John, who formed a meaningful connection with a shelter resident named Mike. Through John's encouragement and support, Mike found stable employment and housing. This story highlights the transformative power of community service.

Consider the story of a retired couple, Maria and David, who dedicated their time to mentoring at-risk youth. Through their guidance and support, many young individuals were able to overcome challenges and achieve their goals. One memorable story involves a young man named Alex, who, with Maria and David's mentorship, graduated from college and started his own business. Their story illustrates the profound impact that community service and mentorship can have on individuals' lives.

A heartwarming example of community service comes from a local business that partnered with a non-profit organization to provide job training and employment opportunities for individuals with disabilities. The program's success stories included individuals who, after completing the training, secured fulfilling jobs and gained independence. This partnership not only benefited the participants but also enriched the company's culture and strengthened its ties to the community.

11

Chapter 11: The Role of Mentorship in Personal Development

Mentorship is a valuable tool for personal and professional growth. It involves sharing knowledge, experience, and guidance to help others achieve their potential. One notable story is that of a seasoned entrepreneur, Jane, who took a young aspiring business owner, Alex, under her wing. Through regular meetings and advice, Jane helped Alex navigate the challenges of starting a new venture. Alex's business thrived, and he later became a mentor to others, continuing the cycle of support and growth.

In another instance, a teacher named Mr. Thompson recognized a student's talent for mathematics and provided extra coaching and encouragement. The student, Emily, excelled in her studies and went on to pursue a successful career in engineering. Mr. Thompson's mentorship played a crucial role in shaping Emily's future. This story highlights the importance of recognizing and nurturing potential in others.

Consider the story of a professional organization that implemented a formal mentorship program to support career development. One participant, Mark, was paired with a senior executive, Laura, who provided guidance and insights on leadership and career advancement. Mark's progress and achievements were significantly accelerated through Laura's mentorship. This example demonstrates the benefits of structured mentorship programs in fostering professional growth.

A heartwarming story of mentorship comes from a community center where experienced volunteers mentored young individuals in various skills, from cooking to computer programming. One memorable story involves a young girl named Mia, who learned to code through the mentorship program and later created an app that addressed a community need. Mia's success was made possible by the support and guidance of her mentors, illustrating the transformative power of mentorship.

12

Chapter 12: Balancing Ambition with Ethical Values

Ambition drives success, but it must be balanced with ethical values to ensure long-term fulfillment and positive impact. One inspiring story is that of an inventor named Sam, who developed a groundbreaking medical device. Despite the potential for significant profits, Sam prioritized patient safety and affordability. His commitment to ethical values led to a successful product that improved countless lives and earned him respect in the medical community.

In another instance, a young professional named Rachel aspired to climb the corporate ladder quickly. However, she realized that cutting corners and compromising her values would ultimately undermine her success. Rachel chose to focus on building strong relationships, delivering quality work, and maintaining integrity. Her ethical approach earned her promotions and recognition, proving that ambition and values can coexist harmoniously.

Consider the story of a sports coach who instilled the importance of fair play and sportsmanship in his team. The coach, Mr. Johnson, emphasized that winning was not just about the score but also about how the game was played. One memorable story involves a match where the team had the opportunity to win through a technicality, but they chose to compete fairly instead. Their decision not only earned them the respect of their opponents but also reinforced the values of integrity and sportsmanship.

A heartwarming example of balancing ambition with ethical values comes from a young artist named Lily, who gained fame for her unique and expressive artwork. Despite offers from commercial entities to mass-produce her art, Lily chose to maintain the authenticity and originality of her work. She continued to create meaningful pieces that resonated with her audience, proving that success does not require compromising one's values.

13

Chapter 13: The Power of Gratitude

Gratitude is a powerful force that can enhance well-being and relationships. It involves recognizing and appreciating the positive aspects of life and expressing thanks to others. One inspiring story is that of a successful entrepreneur, John, who always made it a point to thank his employees and acknowledge their contributions. His genuine gratitude created a positive work environment, motivating his team to perform at their best. John's story highlights the impact of gratitude in fostering a supportive and productive workplace.

In another instance, a teacher named Mrs. Lee implemented a gratitude journal in her classroom, encouraging students to write down things they were thankful for each day. The practice improved the students' mood and overall classroom atmosphere. One memorable story involves a student, Mia, who initially struggled with self-esteem but, through the gratitude journal, learned to appreciate her strengths and achievements. This example illustrates the transformative power of gratitude in personal development.

Consider the story of a community that organized a "Thank You" event to express gratitude to local service providers, such as firefighters, teachers, and healthcare workers. The event not only showed appreciation for their efforts but also strengthened the bonds within the community. One touching story involves a firefighter, David, who was moved by the heartfelt messages from residents and felt a renewed sense of purpose in his work. This story demonstrates the positive impact of expressing gratitude on both individuals and communities.

A heartwarming example of gratitude comes from a family that experienced a health crisis. When their mother, Sarah, was hospitalized, friends and neighbors rallied to provide meals, support, and encouragement. The family expressed their deep gratitude through handwritten thank-you notes and a community gathering. This act of appreciation not only strengthened their relationships but also created a lasting sense of solidarity and support within the community.

14

Chapter 14: The Importance of Work-Life Balance

Maintaining a healthy work-life balance is essential for overall well-being and success. It involves prioritizing both professional responsibilities and personal fulfillment. One notable story is that of a successful lawyer, Jane, who realized that her demanding career was taking a toll on her health and family life. Jane made a conscious effort to set boundaries and allocate time for self-care and family activities. Her improved work Her improved work-life balance not only enhanced her health and relationships but also increased her productivity and job satisfaction. Jane's story underscores the importance of finding harmony between work and personal life for long-term success and well-being.

In another instance, a tech executive named Mark realized that his long hours were affecting his relationship with his family. Determined to make a change, Mark implemented flexible working hours and remote work options for himself and his team. This shift allowed employees to better manage their work and personal commitments. One memorable story involves an employee, Sarah, who was able to attend her child's school events without compromising her work performance. Mark's initiative demonstrates the positive impact of work-life balance on employee well-being and organizational success.

Consider the story of a small business owner, Anna, who struggled to find time for her hobbies and passions due to her demanding schedule. Realizing the importance of self-care, Anna decided to delegate tasks and prioritize activities that brought her joy. This change not only improved her mental health but also inspired her team to pursue their own interests outside of work. Anna's story highlights the benefits of work-life balance in achieving personal fulfillment and maintaining a healthy mindset.

A heartwarming example of work-life balance comes from a couple, John and Lisa, who ran a family-owned café. They made it a priority to spend quality time with their children and each other, despite their busy work schedules. By involving their children in the business and planning regular family outings, they created a strong bond and a supportive environment. John and Lisa's story shows that work-life balance is achievable and can lead to a happier and more connected family life.

15

Chapter 15: Inspiring the Next Generation

Inspiring the next generation to uphold moral values, faith, and business acumen is a vital legacy. It involves being a positive role model and mentor for young people. One notable story is that of a teacher named Mrs. Clark, who dedicated her career to instilling a love of learning and ethical values in her students. Through her passion and dedication, Mrs. Clark inspired many students to pursue their dreams and make a positive impact on society. One memorable story involves a former student, Alex, who returned to the school as a motivational speaker, sharing his success story and encouraging students to strive for excellence.

In another instance, a successful entrepreneur named David took on the role of a mentor for young aspiring business owners. He organized workshops and seminars to share his knowledge and experience, providing valuable insights and guidance. One of his mentees, Maria, went on to establish a thriving business that adhered to ethical practices and contributed to her community. David's mentorship and support played a crucial role in Maria's success, highlighting the importance of passing on knowledge and values to the next generation.

Consider the story of a community leader, Mr. Johnson, who founded a youth center to provide a safe and supportive environment for young people.

The center offered various programs, from sports to arts, aimed at fostering personal growth and development. One heartwarming story involves a young boy named Liam, who discovered his passion for music through the center's programs. With the support and encouragement of Mr. Johnson and the center's staff, Liam pursued his musical dreams and eventually became a professional musician. This example demonstrates the power of community support in inspiring and nurturing the next generation.

A touching example of inspiring the next generation comes from a grandmother, Mrs. Thompson, who shared her life experiences and wisdom with her grandchildren. Through storytelling and personal anecdotes, she taught them the importance of morals, faith, and resilience. One memorable story involves her granddaughter, Emily, who faced a challenging situation and drew strength from her grandmother's lessons. Emily's success in overcoming the challenge is a testament to the enduring impact of Mrs. Thompson's guidance. This story illustrates the profound influence that family members can have in shaping the values and future of young individuals.

Description: Guiding Light: Teaching Morals, Faith, and Business Acumen to the Next Generation:

Guiding Light: Teaching Morals, Faith, and Business Acumen to the Next Generation is an inspiring and enlightening journey into the heart of what it means to lead a life filled with purpose, integrity, and compassion. This book is a treasure trove of wisdom, offering readers practical guidance on instilling essential values and skills in the next generation.

Through engaging stories and thoughtful reflections, **Guiding Light** explores the core principles that shape our moral compass, from honesty and empathy to faith and resilience. Each chapter delves into a different aspect of personal and professional growth, providing valuable insights and real-life examples that illustrate the transformative power of these values.

Readers will be captivated by the tales of individuals who have overcome adversity, led with humility, and made ethical decisions that have positively impacted their communities. Whether it's a young entrepreneur navigating the challenges of starting a business, or a teacher instilling a love of learning and ethical values in her students, each story is a testament to the enduring power of character and determination.

Guiding Light also emphasizes the importance of lifelong learning, work-life balance, and community service, encouraging readers to continually strive for personal growth and to make a difference in the world around them. By weaving together personal anecdotes, inspirational stories, and practical advice, this book serves as a beacon of hope and guidance for anyone looking to lead a meaningful and impactful life.

Perfect for parents, educators, mentors, and aspiring leaders, **Guiding Light** is a must-read for anyone seeking to nurture the next generation with the values and skills they need to thrive in an ever-changing world. This book is not just a guide; it's a call to action to become the guiding light for others, illuminating the path to a brighter and more ethical future.

www.ingramcontent.com/pod-product-compliance
Lightning Source LLC
LaVergne TN
LVHW020502080526
838202LV00057B/6103